Operationa

CW00589517

Review Exercises

Syllabus version 8

January 2009

HOW TO USE THE REVIEW EXERCISES

Enclosed, you will find review exercises concerning the Introduction to Securities and Investment examination syllabus.

The exercises are designed to help you consolidate and test your knowledge, and to provide a pocket-sized reference to use as part of your final revision.

You will find the correct answer printed on the reverse of each exercise.

Please remember that the exercises are designed to supplement, not replace, the Study Book and Question Bank and Practice Examinations you have also received.

Good luck.

ISBN: 9780 7517 7132 9

© BPP Learning Media Ltd – January 2009

£20.00

Exercise

What are the three common categories of risk?	■ ■ ■
What are the consequences of an aircraft crash?	■ ■ ■ ■
What is the general definition of risk?	
What is another name for chance?	

Answer

What are the three common categories of risk?	■ Credit risk. ■ Market risk. ■ Operational risk.
What are the consequences of an aircraft crash?	■ Loss of passenger/aircrew lives. ■ Financial loss arising from the destruction of the aircraft. ■ Financial loss arising from the consequential litigation. ■ Damage to reputation.
What is the general definition of risk?	The hazard or chance of bad consequences or loss occurring.
What is another name for chance?	Probability.

BPP
LEARNING MEDIA

Exercise

What is another name for bad consequences?	
What are examples of everyday risk?	■ ■ ■
What is the definition of risk management?	
What are the four important aspects of the description of risk management?	■ ■ ■ ■

Answer

What is another name for bad consequences?	Negative outcome or downside risk.
What are examples of everyday risk?	■ Betting. ■ Road accidents. ■ Examinations.
What is the definition of risk management?	The implementation of a structured process that reduces the likelihood of risks being realised to acceptable levels.
What are the four important aspects of the description of risk management?	■ Implementation. ■ A structured process. ■ Reduces the likelihood. ■ Acceptable levels.

Exercise

Can we apply risk management to everyday risks – horse racing?	
Can we apply risk management to everyday risks – road accidents?	
Can we apply risk management to everyday risks – examinations?	
How can we define 'risk measurement'?	

Answer

Can we apply risk management to everyday risks – horse racing?	Researching past form, odds offered and track condition knowledge help taking the decision on which horse to bet on.
Can we apply risk management to everyday risks – road accidents?	Speed limits and road signs are designed to reduce the risks of driving.
Can we apply risk management to everyday risks – examinations?	The potential of failure is reduced by revision.
How can we define 'risk measurement'?	By answering the questions ■ What is the probability that the risk will be realised (occur)? ■ How severe will the impact be if the risk is realised? Measurement is objective.

Exercise

Is risk assessment different from risk measurement and, if so, how?	
Why do we measure risk?	
What is the BIS definition of operational risk?	

Answer

Is risk assessment different from risk measurement and, if so, how?	Risk assessment is more to do with estimating the impact the risk has on the business, rather than the probability of the risk being realised. It is subjective.
Why do we measure risk?	By knowing the potential size of a problem and how often it is expected to occur, it is possible to take effective preventative measures and design optimal strategies to manage the events.
What is the BIS definition of operational risk?	The risk of direct or indirect loss resulting from inadequate or failed internal processes, people and systems or from external events.

Exercise

What is strategic risk?	
What is business risk?	
What is legal risk?	

Answer

What is strategic risk?	The risk of loss due to a sub-optimal strategy being employed. It is associated with the way that the business is managed.
What is business risk?	The risk that losses may occur due to an adverse external environment such as high inflation, higher competition, or legal, tax or regulatory changes.
What is legal risk?	The risk due to the losses incurred from legal issues such as being sued, customer compensation or failure to enforce contracts or collateral.

Exercise

Of legal, strategic and business risk, which can be defined as part of operational risk?	
What are the internal processes where operational risk exists?	■ ■ ■ ■ ■ ■ ■ ■
What are the three principal concerns of operational risk?	■ ■ ■

Answer

Introduction to Operational Risk

Of legal, strategic and business risk, which can be defined as part of operational risk?	As far as the BIS is concerned, only legal risk.
What are the internal processes where operational risk exists?	■ Dealing. ■ Marketing and selling. ■ Operations. ■ Legal. ■ Credit. ■ Accounting. ■ IT and project functions. ■ Human resources.
What are the three principal concerns of operational risk?	■ Identifying risk. ■ Measuring risk. ■ Mitigating risk.

Exercise

What were the reasons behind the collapse of Enron?	■
	■
	■
	■

Answer

Enron: the causes

What were the reasons behind the collapse of Enron?	<ul><li>Mismanagement and mistreatment of shareholders</li><li>Allegation of fraud against staff</li><li>Auditors instructing the destruction of documentary evidence</li><li>Growth/share price dependent on dubious accounting practice</li></ul>

Exercise

What is the definition of credit risk?	
How does credit risk sub-divide for on-balance sheet transactions?	
How does credit risk sub-divide for off-balance sheet transactions?	
What is credit exposure?	

Answer

What is the definition of credit risk?	Credit risk or 'default' risk is the loss caused by the failure of a counterparty to pay its obligations, i.e. the loss that results from lending.
How does credit risk sub-divide for on-balance sheet transactions?	Direct risk where money is lent directly. Issuer risk – where an issuer defaults.
How does credit risk sub-divide for off-balance sheet transactions?	Pre-settlement risk: a risk that an institution defaults prior to settlement. Settlement risk: where there is a non-simultaneous exchange between counterparties.
What is credit exposure?	The amount that can potentially be lost if a debtor defaults. It can be used for both individual counterparties and portfolios of exposures.

Exercise

What is the difference between current and potential exposure?	
Who are the three main credit ratings agencies?	■ ■ ■
What is a credit risk premium?	
Does this change over time?	

Answer

What is the difference between current and potential exposure?	Current is what you are owed now. Potential exposure is the calculation of the likely maximum loss in the event of a default. This is usually established using statistical techniques.
Who are the three main credit ratings agencies?	■ Standard & Poor's. ■ Moody's Investor Services. ■ Fitch Ratings.
What is a credit risk premium?	The difference between the risk (default) free rate, and the rate that any specific customer pays to borrow or issue debt.
Does this change over time?	Yes – as the firm's credit risk changes for the worse, the market will demand a higher risk premium and vice versa.

Exercise

What two statistical tools can we use to measure credit risk?	■
	■
Which are the common assumptions used in credit modelling that can lead to inaccuracy?	■
	■
	■
	■

Answer

What two statistical tools can we use to measure credit risk?	■ PD – Probability of default ■ LGD – Loss given default.
Which are the common assumptions used in credit modelling that can lead to inaccuracy?	■ Using simplified calculations of potential exposure. Potential exposure is generally greater than current exposure. Notional amounts are not always good guides to future exposures. ■ Assuming that some exposures have the same credit risk, i.e. comparing an Argentinian Bank Credit with a Spanish Bank Credit. ■ A lack of recognition of the time period of credit risk. Default risk increases with the time of the exposure. ■ Not taking into consideration the moderating effect of portfolio diversification.

Exercise

What are the four methods of mitigating credit risk at the individual level, i.e. specific borrowers?	■ ■ ■ ■
What is perfected collateral?	
What are the three methods of clearing collateral?	■ ■ ■

21

Answer

Mitigating Credit Risk

What are the four methods of mitigating credit risk at the individual level, i.e. specific borrowers?	■ Underwriting standards (quality of credit assessment). ■ Credit limits. ■ Netting. ■ Collateral or margin.
What is perfected collateral?	Where the party providing the collateral retains ownership, but the party taking the collateral is given certain rights to take possession given the default of the party providing it (i.e. their default).
What are the three methods of clearing collateral?	■ Unilateral – where only one party gives collateral to the other. ■ Bilateral – where both parties might post collateral against future potential exposures. ■ Netted agreement – where the net obligation between two parties is collateralised by the obligor only.

Exercise

What is the definition of an efficient portfolio?	
What are the four common techniques for establishing efficient portfolios?	■ ■ ■ ■
Who will be the suppliers of the resources to enable a central counterparty (clearing house) to fulfil its liabilities?	
What does a clearing house require from those transacting business on the exchange being cleared?	

Answer

What is the definition of an efficient portfolio?	It provides the greatest expected return for a given level of risk, or it provides the lowest risk for a given level of expected return.
What are the four common techniques for establishing efficient portfolios?	■ Portfolio diversification. ■ Asset securitisation. ■ Loan sales. ■ Credit derivatives.
Who will be the suppliers of the resources to enable a central counterparty (clearing house) to fulfil its liabilities?	■ Their members. ■ The exchange that is being cleared. ■ Other parties with no direct relationship, i.e. an insurance company or a group of underwriting banks
What does a clearing house require from those transacting business on the exchange being cleared?	■ Initial margin, which remains with the clearing house for the life of the contract. ■ Variation margin, which reflects the daily profit or loss.

Exercise

What are the three purposes of credit derivatives?	■
	■
	■
What are the three types of credit derivative?	■
	■
	■

Answer

Credit Derivatives

What are the three purposes of credit derivatives?	■ To mitigate the credit risk more effectively and improve portfolio diversification by reducing undesirable credit risk concentrations.
	■ To customise the credit exposure to another counterparty without having a direct relationship with them.
	■ To transfer credit risk without adversely affecting customer relations.
What are the three types of credit derivative?	■ Credit default swap.
	■ Total return swap.
	■ Credit-linked notes.

Exercise

What is the definition of market risk?	
How can market risk be sub-divided?	■ ■ ■ ■

Answer

What is the definition of market risk?	The risk of loss of earnings or capital arising from changes in the value of financial instruments.
How can market risk be sub-divided?	■ Price level risk ■ Volatility risk. ■ Liquidity risk. ■ Basis risk.

Exercise

How does a VaR model work?	
Does a normal VaR give you a worst case scenario of loss?	
How do you find out if your VaR model is working given normal market conditions?	
What are the advantages of using a VaR model?	■ ■ ■

Answer

How does a VaR model work?	It applies a given confidence level to the potential changes in the values of the assets over a given period (holding period). This is mostly achieved by applying historic data to potential future changes.
Does a normal VaR give you a worst case scenario of loss?	No. You need to carry out a separate 'Stress Test' to establish the worst case scenario.
How do you find out if your VaR model is working given normal market conditions?	You carry out ongoing back tests. These allow you to see how many times the predicted loss is exceeded, thus establishing whether this falls within the designed confidence level.
What are the advantages of using a VaR model?	■ It provides a statistical probability of potential loss.
	■ It can make an assessment of the correlation between different assets.
	■ It translates all risks in a portfolio into a common standard – that of potential loss, allowing the quantification of firm-wide aggregated cross product exposures.

Exercise

What are the disadvantages of a VaR model?	■
	■
	■
What are three ways of mitigating market risk?	■
	■
	■
What is the downside of hedging using similar, but not the same, assets?	■
	■
	■

Answer

What are the disadvantages of a VaR model?	■ It cannot account for liquidity risk. ■ It is dependent on good historical data. ■ For cash it is less useful for medium or long-term exposures.
What are three ways of mitigating market risk?	■ Hedging. ■ Diversification. ■ Applying risk limits to trading positions.
What is the downside of hedging using similar, but not the same assets?	■ You retain basis risk – the assets may not move at the same speed. ■ You may enter into greater credit risk. ■ You will almost certainly enter into more operational risk.

Exercise

Name the elements of a good practice risk management framework?	■ ■ ■ ■ ■ ■

Answer

Effective Market Risk Management

Name the elements of a good practice risk management framework?	<ul><li>An independent daily monitoring function of risk utilisation through the daily production of profit and loss accounts, and independent review of front office closing prices.</li><li>Proactive management involvement in risk issues.</li><li>Defined escalation policies to deal with rising levels of trading loss, which include risk limits.</li><li>VaR as a common measure of risk exposure.</li><li>A clearly defined risk management policy.</li><li>Independent validation of market pricing and adequacy of VaR models.</li></ul>

Exercise

If you use a VaR model, what are the three requirements for producing the model for regulatory capital purposes?	■
	■
	■

Answer

VaR: Regulatory Requirements

If you use a VaR model, what are the three requirements for producing the model for regulatory capital purposes?	■ You should use not less than 250 days (one year) historic data. ■ You should use a 99% confidence level. ■ You should use a ten-day holding period.

Exercise

What is the chain of events in operational risk?	
What is involved in operations risk?	■ ■ ■ ■ ■ ■
What is an organisation's corporate culture?	

Answer

What is the chain of events in operational risk?	Root cause followed by Internal events followed by consequences or effects or impacts.
What is involved in operations risk?	■ Transaction capture. ■ Confirmation. ■ Trade instructions. ■ Positioning. ■ Settlement. ■ Reconciliation.
What is an organisation's corporate culture?	The collective norms and values of its employees

Exercise

Risk Culture: The Role Of Management

What are the four main issues that impact the risk culture?	■ ■ ■ ■
What is the effect of leadership on corporate culture?	
What responsibilities do senior managers have regarding operational risk management?	■ ■ ■ ■

Answer

What are the four main issues that impact the risk culture?	■ Quality and integrity of staff. ■ How much an organisation changes. ■ The effectiveness of the control environment. ■ Reward practices.
What is the effect of leadership on corporate culture?	Leadership dictates the formation of a corporate culture.
What responsibilities do senior managers have regarding operational risk management?	■ Awareness of operational risk. ■ Approval and review of operational risk framework. ■ Ensure this framework is independently audited. ■ Ensure segregation is maintained between internal audit and operational risk management.

Exercise

What actions are required to create and maintain a favourable risk culture?	■
	■
	■
	■
	■
	■
	■
	■
	■

Answer

What actions are required to create and maintain a favourable risk culture?	<ul><li>High degree of personal responsibility.</li><li>Individual motivation to promote effort, care and commitment.</li><li>Boost morale.</li><li>Promote high levels of integrity.</li><li>Create an appropriate environment to manage operational risk.</li><li>Continually measure performance against targets.</li><li>Collective risk awareness.</li><li>Manage change.</li><li>Ensure staff have the correct level of technical ability and experience.</li></ul>

Exercise

What are the two key objectives of operational risk management?	■ ■
What is the risk management process?	■ ■ ■ ■ ■ ■
What are the seven areas addressed by operational risk policy?	■ ■ ■ ■ ■ ■ ■

Answer

Operational Risk Management

What are the two key objectives of operational risk management?	■ Gaining an understanding of the operational risks faced by a firm that could prevent it from meeting its strategic objectives. ■ Implementing a firm-wide approach to combat these risks.
What is the risk management process?	■ Risk identification. ■ Risk measurement and assessment. ■ Risk mitigation. ■ Risk monitoring. ■ Risk reporting. ■ Operational risk policy.
What are the seven areas addressed by operational risk policy?	■ Identify key-risk officers. ■ Consistency. ■ Responsibility and accountability. ■ Collaboration between divisions. ■ Co-ordination. ■ Sponsorship. ■ Segregation of duties.

Exercise

Risk Identification (1)

Why is it useful to identify risks?	■
	■
	■
	■
	■

Answer

Why is it useful to identify risks?	<ul><li>To provide information to management on which to make decisions.</li><li>To establish the chain of events relationship of operational risk and understand where they occur throughout the firm.</li><li>To provide a basis of risk measurement and assessment.</li><li>To differentiate between operational risk and other types of risk.</li><li>To develop common language for discussion, assessing and managing risk that allows clear and transparent communication and decision making.</li></ul>

Exercise

What are the most commonly used methods of identification of operational risks?	■ ■ ■ ■
Is self-assessment subjective or objective?	
Can risk audits be carried out by normal internal auditors?	
What are the key points of focus workshops for assessing operational risk?	■ ■ ■ ■ ■

47

Answer

What are the most commonly used methods of identification of operational risks?	■ Self-assessment. ■ Reviews/audits. ■ Focus workshops. ■ Historical loss analysis.
Is self-assessment subjective or objective?	Subjective
Can risk audits be carried out by normal internal auditors?	Not really, they should be carried out by expert analysts trained in operational risk methodology.
What are the key points of focus workshops for assessing operational risk?	■ They engage all of the relevant risk owners at the same time. ■ They analyse the end to end chain of events. ■ They investigate cross-functional awareness. ■ They become the catalysts for change. ■ Raise risk awareness.

Exercise

What are the practical problems of risk identification?	■
	■
	■
	■

Answer

Risk Identification (3)

What are the practical problems of risk identification?	■ The amount of time it takes for managers and staff to ensure it is done properly.
	■ The lack of good quality, consistent historical data.
	■ The lack of mature policies and methods of collecting and compiling a risk profile.
	■ Difficulties in adequately categorising risk data.

Exercise

Why bother to measure risk?	■
	■
	■
	■
	■
	■
	■

Answer

Why bother to measure risk?	<ul><li>To gain an understanding of the size and cost of impact that the risk has on the business.</li><li>To establish a quantitative baseline for improving the risk environment.</li><li>To ensure there is appropriate accountability for risk management.</li><li>To provide an incentive for risk management and the development of a risk aware culture.</li><li>To improve management decision making by knowing the size of the risks that they face.</li><li>To satisfy regulators and shareholders that firm is proactive on risk management.</li><li>To make an assessment of the financial risk exposure that can be used for capital adequacy purposes.</li></ul>

Exercise

Measuring Risk (2)

What are the seven subjective methods of measuring risk?	■ ■ ■ ■ ■ ■ ■
When using a ranking methodology, what two elements must be included?	■ ■
What is the formula to establish the level of risk?	

Answer

What are the six subjective methods of measuring risk?	■ Ranking and assessing. ■ Self-assessment. ■ Scenario analysis ■ Bottom-up approaches. ■ Benchmarking. ■ Using key risk indicators (KRIs). ■ Historical loss data analysis.
When using a ranking methodology, what two elements must be included?	■ The likelihood of the risk being realised. ■ The magnitude of the impact if realised.
What is the formula to establish the level of risk?	Risk = Likelihood (%) × Magnitude of impact (£)

Exercise

What are the advantages of ranking?	■
	■
	■
	■
	■
	■
Are there any disadvantages in ranking?	

Answer

What are the advantages of ranking?	■ It provides a simple method of viewing a range of risks faced by the unit in question.
	■ It focuses management attention on the most important risks.
	■ It can be used with minimal hard data so, if historical data is not available, useful measurement can still be achieved.
	■ It can capture a wide range of risk possibilities from large to detailed. It can thus be effective at all levels of an organisation.
	■ It can be used to anticipate loss by ranking potential risks of new projects. As a result it is useful in periods of change.
	■ It encourages a risk aware culture and a more transparent risk environment.
Are there any disadvantages in ranking?	It tends to be subjective, and may present an oversimplified view.

Exercise

What are the limitations of self-assessment?	■
	■
	■
	■
How does scenario analysis work?	

Answer

What are the limitations of self-assessment?	■ It is subjective. ■ It can be open to abuse and manipulation by managers. ■ It can be difficult to apply consistently across the various business units and multiple locations that exist within a global investment bank. ■ It is more effective when used in conjunction with other methodologies.
How does scenario analysis work?	It is very similar to stress testing in VaR models, whereby a series of possible scenarios are imposed upon the business, and the downside is measured.

Exercise

What are the advantages of bottom-up measurement approaches?	■
	■
	■
	■
	■

Answer

What are the advantages of bottom-up measurement approaches?	■ They address risk and control issues at the process level, so complement the role of line managers.
	■ The accountability and responsibility for risk management can be clearly defined. The manager of a process is usually made accountable for managing the risks it contains.
	■ It encourages a risk aware culture and a more transparent risk environment.
	■ It encourages a continuous improvement approach to risk management. This means that improvements to the control environment can be made quickly in the short term.
	■ It improves the quality of management information.

Exercise

What are the disadvantages of bottom-up measurement approaches?	■ ■ ■
What are the advantages of benchmarking?	■ ■
What are the disadvantages of benchmarking?	■ ■ ■ ■

Answer

What are the disadvantages of bottom-up measurement approaches?	■ It takes time to implement. ■ Continuing maintenance of risk profiles are frequently major undertakings, particularly in high change environments. ■ It is difficult to apply a consistent set of rules so as to ensure that risks are viewed on a like-for-like basis across separate processes.
What are the advantages of benchmarking?	■ It makes operational risk more transparent within the industry. ■ It allows the firm to make judgements on what 'good' is. It sets a standard for the industry based on the best firm.
What are the disadvantages of benchmarking?	■ It is difficult to find suitable measures that compare like with like. ■ Open and honest reporting of risk measures is difficult to measure. ■ It may create a false sense of security for market leaders. ■ The industry tends to be very secretive.

Exercise

Give some examples of key risk indicators.	■
	■
	■
	■
	■
	■
	■
	■
	■

Answer

Give some examples of key risk indicators.	<ul><li>The number of settlement failures occurring over a given time.</li><li>The number of times a trader exceeds his credit limits.</li><li>The average length of time a confirmation remains unsigned (not returned).</li><li>The mark-to-market value of transactions remaining unconfirmed.</li><li>The number of times funding deadlines are missed in a given time period.</li><li>The number and value of nostro (cash) or depo (position) reconciliation breaks over a specified time period.</li><li>The number of reconciliation breaks between front and back office over a specified time period.</li><li>The value of interest claims incurred over a specified period.</li><li>Number of transactions per head.</li></ul>

Exercise

What are the advantages of KRIs?	■
	■
	■
	■
What are the disadvantages of KRIs?	■
	■
	■
What are the four risk mitigation strategies?	■
	■
	■
	■

Answer

What are the advantages of KRIs?	■ They allow trends to be monitored. ■ They allow limits of acceptability to be established. ■ They provide a basis for objective performance measurement. ■ They act as early warning signals.
What are the disadvantages of KRIs?	■ They can be misleading if used in isolation. ■ They are difficult to obtain automatically. ■ They are prone to manipulation.
What are the four risk mitigation strategies?	■ Reduce the likelihood. ■ Reduce the impact. ■ Avoid the risk. ■ Transfer the risk.

Exercise

What are the two categories of controls to reduce the likelihood of risk?	■ ■
What are the available strategies to reduce the impact of operational risk?	■ ■ ■ ■ ■ ■
What can you do to transfer the risk?	

Answer

Risk Mitigation

What are the two categories of controls to reduce the likelihood of risk?	■ Preventative controls. ■ Detective controls.
What are the available strategies to reduce the impact of operational risk?	■ Diversification. ■ Risk sharing. ■ Financial provisioning. ■ Contingency planning. ■ Good communication and reporting. ■ Limit setting.
What can you do to transfer the risk?	Take insurance or outsource.

Exercise

What are the five functions of risk reporting?	■
	■
	■
	■
	■
What are the four principles of good practice for risk reporting?	■
	■
	■
	■

Answer

What are the five functions of risk reporting?	■ To provide transparency of risk status and issues. ■ To aid communication. ■ To reduce uncertainty. ■ To allow early, decisive action to address the risks. ■ To escalate issues and recommendations.
What are the four principles of good practice for risk reporting?	Good reporting should be ■ Timely. ■ Accurate. ■ Informative. ■ Explanatory.

Exercise

What in essence does the New Basel Capital Accord propose?	
What are the three pillars of the New Accord?	■ ■ ■

Answer

The New Basel Accord (1)

What in essence does the New Basel Capital Accord propose?	That all measurable risk should be measured, with an appropriate level of capital required to drive those risks. These risks will be sub-divided into three: market, credit and operational.
What are the three pillars of the New Accord?	Pillar 1 ■ A requirement to demonstrate minimum capital. Pillar 2 ■ The supervisory review process – The encouragement of institutions by supervisors to better measure the risks. Pillar 3 ■ Market discipline – The requirement that institutions provide much wider disclosure of levels, types and degree of risks held within their books

Exercise

How is the capital ratio to be measured?	
What are the three common measurement standards?	■ ■ ■

Answer

How is the capital ratio to be measured?	Capital ratio = Capital requirement ÷ (Credit risk exposure + Market risk exposure + Operational risk exposure)
What are the three common measurement standards?	■ Basic indicator approach. ■ Standardised approach. ■ Advanced measurement approach (AMA).

Exercise

What are the two basic consequences of operational risk?	■ ■
What are direct consequences due to?	■ ■ ■ ■ ■ ■

Answer

What are the two basic consequences of operational risk?	■ Direct (quantifiable) financial loss. ■ Indirect (non-quantifiable) financial loss.
What are direct consequences due to?	■ Claims for damages as a result of failure to meet contractual obligations. ■ Penalties from regulatory censure or revocation of licences. ■ Loss of income from transaction fees and commissions. ■ Loss of assets or cash through unenforceable contracts. ■ Associated direct cost of rectifying mistakes that led to the loss. ■ Corrections to P&L due to errors in booking transactions.

Exercise

What are the indirect consequences due to?	■ ■ ■
What are the root causes of operational risk?	■ ■ ■ ■
What are the process causes?	■ ■ ■ ■ ■

Answer

What are the indirect consequences due to?	■ A lack of operational capability. ■ Damage to the firm's reputation by adverse publicity on unsuitable clients, perceived malpractice, public dispute with customers, poor customer service resulting in loss of future business opportunities. ■ Associated costs of correcting the operational problem.
What are the root causes of operational risk?	■ Processes. ■ People. ■ Technology. ■ Environment.
What are the process causes?	■ A lack of effective procedures. ■ A lack of capacity. ■ Volume sensitivity. ■ A lack of effective controls. ■ A failure to review controls.

Exercise

What are the people causes of operational risk?	<ul><li></li><li></li><li></li><li></li><li></li><li></li><li></li><li></li><li></li><li></li></ul>

Answer

What are the people causes of operational risk?	<ul><li>Human error.</li><li>Staff acting in an unauthorised fashion.</li><li>A lack of accountability of operational risk management.</li><li>A lack of integrity and honesty leading to fraud or theft.</li><li>A lack of customer care.</li><li>A lack of skills and/or insufficient training.</li><li>Poor communication.</li><li>Concentration of expertise.</li><li>A lack of supervision.</li><li>Lack of an effective control culture.</li></ul>

Exercise

Technology Causes of Operational Risk

What are the technology causes of operational risk?	■
	■
	■
	■
	■
	■

Answer

What are the technology causes of operational risk?	<ul><li>A lack of system availability caused by</li></ul>
	<ul><li>– Poor design.</li><li>– Inadequate security.</li><li>– Power failures.</li><li>– Fire, flood, lightning etc.</li></ul>
	<ul><li>A lack of system integrity. If there is no electronic passage of data there is a requirement for</li></ul>
	<ul><li>– Manual rekeying.</li><li>– Reconciliation between systems.</li></ul>
	<ul><li>Inadequate control functionality driven by desire to reduce costs rather than properly control the business.</li></ul>
	<ul><li>Inadequate system testing.</li></ul>
	<ul><li>Lack of strategic approach to system design.</li></ul>
	<ul><li>High system complexity rendering it difficult to change or integrate.</li></ul>

Exercise

What are the environmental causes of operational risk?	■
	■
	■
	■
	■
	■
	■

Answer

What are the environmental causes of operational risk?	<ul><li>War, terrorism and natural disasters.</li><li>Regulatory and/or tax changes.</li><li>The use of new technology.</li><li>The acceleration of volume increases.</li><li>Lack of staff availability leading to higher staff costs/lower staff ability.</li><li>The ever increasing rationalisation of the industry.</li><li>The pace of change.</li></ul>

Exercise

What are the internal effects of operational risk?	■ ■ ■ ■ ■ ■ ■
Why can data be incorrect?	■ ■
What are the consequences of incorrect data?	■ ■ ■

Answer

Internal Effects of Operational Risk

What are the internal effects of operational risk?	<ul><li>Incorrect data.</li><li>Delayed processing.</li><li>Regulatory non-compliance.</li><li>Project failure.</li><li>Poor customer service.</li><li>Fraud and theft.</li><li>Unforeseen litigation.</li></ul>
Why can data be incorrect?	<ul><li>Captured incorrectly.</li><li>It has not been updated to reflect changes in its source.</li></ul>
What are the consequences of incorrect data?	<ul><li>Direct loss due to failed transactions.</li><li>Direct loss if the error is not spotted in time.</li><li>Indirect loss due to damaged reputation as a result of incorrect documentation.</li></ul>

Exercise

What are the consequences of delayed processing?	■ ■ ■
What are the consequences of regulatory non-compliance?	■ ■

Answer

What are the consequences of delayed processing?	■ Direct loss due to a payment or a funding deadline being missed.
	■ Direct loss if the client is lost as a result of delays.
	■ Indirect loss due to damaged reputation as a result of incorrect documentation.
What are the consequences of regulatory non-compliance?	■ Direct loss through fines.
	■ Indirect loss through regulatory censure, with resulting damage to reputation.

Exercise

What are the consequences of project failure?	■
	■
	■
	■
	■
	■
	■

Answer

What are the consequences of project failure?	■ Direct loss through the need to use more resources to bring a delayed project back on line.
	■ Direct loss through project delays creating higher costs.
	■ Direct loss through cancelling a project halfway through implementation.
	■ Direct loss through having to set up further projects to sort out an inadequate solution.
	■ Indirect loss through lost opportunity to use resources tied up in failed projects.
	■ Indirect loss through the destabilising influence of project demands on staff time.
	■ Indirect loss through an uncoordinated or inadequately controlled system change resulting in a change beyond the firm's capacity.

Exercise

What is the life cycle of a transaction?	■
	■
	■
	■
	■
What takes place at the set-up phase?	■
	■
	■
	■

Operational Risk Cycle (1)

What is the life cycle of a transaction?	■ Set-up phase. ■ Trade execution. ■ Pre-settlement phase. ■ Settlement. ■ Post-settlement phase.
What takes place at the set-up phase?	■ Establishing and maintaining customer relationships. ■ Negotiating legal agreements. ■ Assessing credit risk, creditworthiness and establishing credit limits. ■ Setting up and sourcing all data required by the processing systems to process the transaction, such as new instruments, price information, credit information, customer details and settlement instructions (static data).

Exercise

Operational Risk Cycle (2)

What takes place at the execution phase?	■ ■ ■ ■
What takes place at the post-settlement phase?	■ ■ ■

Answer

What takes place at the execution phase?	■ Trade booking. ■ Monitoring settlement events. ■ Monitoring credit and position limits. ■ Financial and regulatory reporting.
What takes place at the post-settlement phase?	■ Processing the movement of assets. ■ Inventory management – managing custody and corporate events. ■ Reconciliation of internal records to the outside world.

Exercise

What part of the life cycle of a transaction is covered by market and credit risk?	
What part of the life cycle of a transaction is covered by operational risk?	
What are the eight major functions within a bank that contribute to the management of risk?	■ ■ ■ ■ ■ ■ ■ ■

Answer

What part of the life cycle of a transaction is covered by market and credit risk?	Market and credit risk only start once the deal is transacted, and continue until the deal finally matures.
What part of the life cycle of a transaction is covered by operational risk?	Operational risk covers the entire lifecycle from set up until final maturity. A deal like an interest rate swap will continue to have operational risk until its final payments are exchanged.
What are the eight major functions within a bank that contribute to the management of risk?	<ul><li>Compliance.</li><li>Audit.</li><li>Legal.</li><li>Credit.</li><li>Accounting.</li><li>IT and project functions.</li><li>Human resources.</li><li>Marketing.</li></ul>

Exercise

What are the objectives of the Compliance department?	■ ■ ■
What is regarded as good practice in compliance?	■ ■ ■ ■
What do the regulators demand from the Compliance department?	■ ■ ■ ■

Answer

What are the objectives of the Compliance department?	■ Good corporate governance. ■ Organisational integrity. ■ Regulatory compliance by defining the programmes and processes that ensure compliance to the regulations.
What is regarded as good practice in compliance?	■ Advising on supervisory matters. ■ Monitoring compliance of rules. ■ Maintaining contact with the regulator. ■ Ensuring that staff are qualified, approved and registered.
What do the regulators demand from the Compliance department?	■ Monthly financial reports. ■ To keep a register of whom is authorised to trade, and what products are traded. ■ Maintenance of custodian and bank nostro details. ■ Keep a register of legal/master agreements.

Exercise

Support and Control Functions (3)

What does the Compliance department do in terms of employees' restrictions?	■
	■
	■
	■
	■
	■
	■
	■

Answer

What does the Compliance department do in terms of employees' restrictions?	■ It polices what deals traders are permitted to carry out on a personal account basis in order to ensure there is no insider trading. ■ It specifies what gifts/ entertainment is acceptable to give/receive. ■ It ensures that whistleblowers are given protection. ■ It overviews the investments made in companies with whom it has professional relationships. ■ It reviews relationships with competitor/reciprocity. ■ It is the media point of contact. ■ It rules on what is or is not confidential. ■ It is responsible for ensuring that all staff are trained in anti-money laundering measures.

Exercise

If compliance is not carried out properly, what are the risks?	■ ■ ■ ■ ■ ■ ■ ■
What is the purpose of internal audit?	■ ■ ■

Answer

If compliance is not carried out properly, what are the risks?	■ Fraud and theft. ■ That staff members trade in stocks that the firm is an insider. ■ That anti-money laundering rules are broken. ■ That limits are broken. ■ That capital adequacy rules are broken. ■ That regulators are mislead or kept uninformed. ■ That dealers trade for their personal account in unauthorised securities. ■ That dealers hide losses (tickets in the drawer!).
What is the purpose of internal audit?	■ To ensure that a firm's business is properly conducted and recorded. ■ To check that the process and procedures are up to date. ■ To ensure that they are in line with policy and documentation.

Exercise

What are nine legal operational risk issues?	■
	■
	■
	■
	■
	■
	■
	■
	■
How does the credit function assess credit risk?	■
	■
	■

Exercise

What are nine legal operational risk issues?	■ Contract formation. ■ Legal names. ■ Jurisdiction. ■ Netting. ■ Collateral or margin. ■ Power to transact. ■ Employee authority. ■ Client relationship. ■ Fiduciary responsibility.
How does the credit function assess credit risk?	■ Looking at ratings prepared by Moody's or Standard & Poor's. ■ Carrying out a full credit analysis. ■ Using quantitative/statistical analysis to assess creditworthiness.

Exercise

What are the operational risk problems associated with credit?	■
	■
	■
	■
What is the difference between internal and external reporting?	

Answer

What are the operational risk problems associated with credit?	■ Poor training of credit analysts leading to invalid assessments. ■ Wrong data/static data leading to breaking credit limits. ■ Misinterpretation of a counterparty's financial statements. ■ Legal risk – the inability to enforce credit-related contracts.
What is the difference between internal and external reporting?	Internal accounting provides information to management in detail on an ongoing basis and is private. External accounting is to provide regulators and investors with information regarding the firm, and is largely public.

Exercise

What are the potential problems of financial reporting?	■
	■
	■
	■
	■
What are the responsibilities of the IT department?	■
	■

Answer

What are the potential problems of financial reporting?	<ul><li>Overestimation of trading profits.</li><li>Misreporting due to aggregation of positions not being correctly handled.</li><li>Traders tend to focus on the future but accountants on the past. This can lead to interdepartmental tensions.</li><li>As accounting standards change, this can lead to misreporting, and confusion.</li><li>As more banks merge, the pressure on the accounting function grows with the stress of integration.</li></ul>
What are the responsibilities of the IT department?	<ul><li>Ensuring that there is consistent system availability.</li><li>Enabling and delivering required change, i.e. STP.</li></ul>

Exercise

What are the responsibilities of the human resources department?	■ ■ ■ ■ ■ ■
What are the responsibilities of the marketing department?	■ ■ ■ ■ ■ ■

Answer

What are the responsibilities of the human resources department?	<ul><li>Recruiting new employees.</li><li>Writing job descriptions.</li><li>Tracking attendance.</li><li>Instituting and monitoring policies and current HR regulations.</li><li>Establishing and maintaining policies and procedures manuals.</li><li>Maintaining employee records.</li></ul>
What are the responsibilities of the marketing department?	<ul><li>Identifying customer needs.</li><li>Creating goods or services.</li><li>Establishing profitable pricing.</li><li>Promotion of goods/services.</li><li>Ensuring promotions meet regulatory requirements.</li><li>Understanding competitors/markets.</li></ul>

Exercise

Integrated Risk Management

What are the objectives of integrated risk management (IRM)?	■ ■ ■
What areas does integrated risk management seek to cover?	■ ■ ■ ■ ■

Answer

What are the objectives of integrated risk management (IRM)?	■ To optimise the overall risk process. ■ To provide an understanding of total risk exposure. ■ To manage the consequences of risk in an integrated manner.
What areas does integrated risk management seek to cover?	■ Market risk. ■ Credit risk. ■ Operational risk. ■ Strategic risk. ■ Business risk.

Exercise

What are the MiFID requirements for the compliance, audit and internal risk functions?	■
	■
	■
	■
	■
	■
	■
	■

Answer

What are the MiFID requirements for the compliance, audit and internal risk functions?	<ul><li>Firms must establish and maintain policies and procedures aimed at ensuring effective compliance.</li><li>Firms must establish procedures that identify risks.</li><li>Firms must assess and address any compliance issues.</li><li>Firms must (normally) have an independent compliance function.</li><li>Firms must appoint a compliance officer.</li><li>If appropriate, firms must establish an internal audit function.</li><li>Firms must establish, implement and maintain adequate risk management policies.</li><li>Firms must have a risk control function, where appropriate, depending on the nature, scale and complexity of its business.</li></ul>